Soul Food
A POET'S FEAST

Soul Food
A POET'S FEAST

Volume One
of the Soul Food Series

MEGAN GREALY

Columbus, Ohio

This book is a work of fiction. The names, characters and events in this book are the products of the author's imagination or are used fictitiously. Any similarity to real persons living or dead is coincidental and not intended by the author.

The views and opinions expressed in this book are solely those of the author and do not reflect the views or opinions of Gatekeeper Press. Gatekeeper Press is not to be held responsible for and expressly disclaims responsibility of the content herein.

A POET'S FEAST

Published by **Gatekeeper Press**
2167 Stringtown Rd, Suite 109
Columbus, OH 43123-2989
www.GatekeeperPress.com

Copyright © 2022 by **Megan Grealy**

All rights reserved. Neither this book, nor any parts within it may be sold or reproduced in any form or by any electronic or mechanical means, including information storage and retrieval systems, without permission in writing from the author. The only exception is by a reviewer, who may quote short excerpts in a review.

The editorial work for this book is entirely the product of the author. Gatekeeper Press did not participate in and is not responsible for any aspect of that element.

Library of Congress Control Number: 2022930375

ISBN (paperback): 9781662922657
eISBN: 9781662922640

CONTENTS

JOY	6
CLEAR	7
ROOT	8
SPIRITS	9
SHIFT	10
THINK	11
SLIP	12
RISE	13
TRACKS	14
RAIN	15
INCEPTION	16
SHEEP	17
FILM	18
FOG	19
NOISE	20
REAL	21
LAVA	22
COMPASS	23
COSMOS	24
SIGHT	25
DIRT	26
SEASONS	27
RAYS	28
WICK	29
FREEZE	30
UNIVERSE	31
BEGIN	32
INNER CHILD	33

JOY

Chills and shivers

up

my

spine.

Growing quicker

than

a

vine.

Sunlight feeling soft like kisses.

Rub my belly, get three wishes.

Wind is sweet like summer rain.

Shining like I've got no pain.

MCG

CLEAR

When I wake the sun is bright.
Kissing me with rays of light.
A   face.
    smile   my
              runs   across

A present moment, a heavenly embrace.
With each deep breath my energy is lifted.
My vision's clear and slightly shifted.

MCG

ROOT

It's like I'm growing with each passing night.

Feeling auric, bright, and light.

Grateful is my favorite color.

Company will start to wonder.

Happiness is heaven on Earth.

Only

you

can sew that worth.

MCG

SPIRITS

Take a sip
they used to say.
Invite the demons in
to play.
Consuming thoughts of exhilaration.
Can't lift my foot from acceleration.
Fluid thoughts of
harmony.
Spirits flowing
endlessly.

MCG

SHIFT

The sand beneath your feet
    quickly starts to shift,
        reminding you of life's
           uncertainty and drift.
Nothing's ever guaranteed and life's
    forever changing.
Embrace the present moment:
    you'll be
forever gaining.

MCG

THINK

what you think

is who you become.

One look in the mirror

and you will run.

your mind is like uncharted land.

Look inside

to understand

what's to say our dreams at night

are any more real than our sight?

MCG

SLIP

I tried to make you happy.
I tried most every day.
I tried to make you understand life's constant disarray.
I cannot take you with me, I cannot bear to watch.
You'd only drive me crazy and turn it up a notch.
It's not the situation; it's how you choose to play.
Not every thought or action deserves a full forte.

The water's getting deeper; it's time for me to go.
I hope you understand, but may not ever know.

MCG

RISE

The fresh air hits me like a brick.

Emotions growing very thick.

I feel as if I've

turned

back

time.

I'd never have to skip a rhyme.

Invest in you and life will rise.

Invest in them and compromise.

MCG

Tracks

I used to care a lot about what others thought.

It never did occur to me; perceptions were just taught.

I turned my focus inward.

I felt a shift in tracks.

An epiphany

for empathy

I just can't seem to lack.

MCG

RAIN

There's something about the

drip

and

drop.

Once it starts it just won't stop.

Cleansing souls, rebirthing rivers.

A fluid cloak to heal my slivers.

MCG

INCEPTION

Thoughts disguised as actions.
Read between the captions.
I need a reaction.
Your time is but a fraction.
Words are nothing but perception.
No one wins this cruel inception.

MCG

SHEEP

The singing grains of sand fall around.

Beating a motion of a drum.

Keeping current like a stock.

Remind me not to flee my flock.

Deep breaths in, just one back out.

Too many sheep,

Too vast to count.

MCG

FILM

Reminiscing. Sipping.
Breeze flowing through.
Smiling about those moments it was
only me and you.
Thoughts won't stop replaying,
running like a film.
You're treasured like new pottery.
Fresh out of the kiln.

MCG

FOG

My golden curls

bounce

and

flow.

The people crying "overthrow".

It's dark outside; come help me see.

The fog's too thick; just let me be.

Vision is among the senses.

Close your eyes to free that penance.

MCG

NOISE

I'm sick of the noise.

I'm sick of the poise.

Dreaming,

floating

mountains high.

Clouds are

lifting in the

sky.

Heaven is a place on Earth.

Present moment, feeling worth.

MCG

REAL

Vision blinding

other senses.

Got me feeling so relentless.

Energy is all I feel.

Humming

through

me

like

a

reel.

MCG

LAVA

I possess some powers
I used to deny.
Look into my eyes and
wonder why.
Magic
oozing
from my pores.
Close your eyes to see my sores.
Splash of water in your face.
Only fate will change your pace.

MCG

COMPASS

In the end, we awake in a field full of flowers.

No sense of time or direction.

No longer searching for affection.

Life is but a reflection.

Searching for connection.

Mind your projection.

Wisdom is loss of direction.

MCG

COSMOS

Reach up for the stars
they say.
Hold on
to the brightest ray.
Neglect
is on the other end.
Reflections
causing light to bend.
The brightest in the
galaxy
is the most authentic
me.

MCG

SIGHT

I could feel your touch
so perfectly.
Didn't need
my eyes
to see.
Powerful electric stream.
Speaking through my soul.
So wise of you to know.

MCG

DIRT

He'll drag you

down.

Rip off your crown.

Run your fingers through the dirt.

Immerse yourself to cleanse the hurt.

Camouflaged to midnight serpents.

Know their trail.

Remain subversive.

MCG

SEASONS

The silence of the night.

I feel it call for me.

I feel it in the way that nature flows through me.

The trees bestow sweet whispers.

I cannot make out what.

The sun provides the strength to pull me from my rut.

The rain is my reminder,

washes off the pain.

The flowers growing taller

remind me of the gain.

MCG

RAYS

I'm waiting for a message in a lantern or a bottle.

A genie would work too.

I can't think of his motto.

The signs are pointing up

to all the work I've done.

The sun is shining brighter.

I'm too far now to run.

I could just stay alone for all my future days.

God's got something special planned.

Reach out and feel his praise.

MCG

WICK

I light a candle every night.

A fiery flame burns oh so bright.

I breathe the scents of winter winds.

I ephale sadness,

defeat, and

sins.

I've built a cocoon to keep me safe.

I tuck in and I pray for faith.

I know this storm will soon pass.

It feels just like an empty glass.

I need a drink- oh so bad,

of fresh ideas and reprimand.

I should be out spreading my wings.

I feel too snug wrapped in my cling.

MCG

FREEZE

protect your energy with all your might
and when you come across a fight
remember who you are and then
close your eyes and count to ten
imagine a gold

and

winding

path

the sun is shining through your chest
beware of evil and deceitful beings
only you can choose your demons.
nothing for you
will pass you by
all you need to do is thrive.

MCG

UNIVERSE

I no longer worry of things
I can't control.
My heart used to be guarded,
always on patrol.
Living in the present moment
is how I pass my time.
Pausing for a moment
just to bust a rhyme.
My fears have lifted.
My worries are gone.
The universe whispers
"what took you so long?".

MCG

BEGIN

Bursting with excitement.
Joy shining through.
The time has now come
for us to see this through.
The journey has been heavy,
but we already knew.
Please lift up the levey
were ready to break through.

MCG

INNER CHILD

Wipe your eyes.
Soften your cries.
Comfort your lies.
Boundaries over compromise.
Feel the fires start to rise.

MCG

www.ingramcontent.com/pod-product-compliance
Lightning Source LLC
LaVergne TN
LVHW020006080526
838200LV00081B/4462